# THE SWEET DAYS DIE

*Poems by William Morris*

Dante Gabriel Rossetti   THE BOWER MEADOW   1872

# THE SWEET DAYS DIE

*Poems by William Morris*

SELECTED AND WITH AN INTRODUCTION BY PAMELA TODD

PAVILION

FOR MY SISTER WITH LOVE

First published in Great Britain in 1996 by

PAVILION BOOKS LIMITED

26 Upper Ground, London SE1 9PD

A CIP catalogue record for this book is available from the British Library

ISBN 1 85793 644  2

Designed by David Fordham

Typeset in Helvetica Bold and Garamond Light by SX Composing Ltd, Rayleigh

Printed and bound in Italy by Graphicom

2 4 6 8 10 9 7 5 3 1

This book may be ordered by post direct from the publisher.

Please contact the Marketing Department. But try your bookshop first.

# CONTENTS

INTRODUCTION . . . . . . . . . . . . . . . . . . . . . 7

THE HOLLOW LAND . . . . . . . . . . . . . . . 12

SUMMER DAWN . . . . . . . . . . . . . . . . . . . 15

SPRING'S BEDFELLOW . . . . . . . . . . . . . . . . 16

FAIR IS THE WORLD . . . . . . . . . . . . . . . . . 17

VERSES FOR PICTURES . . . . . . . . . . . . . . . 18

DRAWING NEAR THE LIGHT . . . . . . . . . . . . . 21

FOR THE BRIAR ROSE . . . . . . . . . . . . . . . . 22

ANOTHER FOR THE BRIAR ROSE . . . . . . . . . . . 24

THE END OF MAY . . . . . . . . . . . . . . . . . . 26

LOVE'S GLEANING-TIDE . . . . . . . . . . . . . . . 29

TWO RED ROSES ACROSS THE MOON . . . . . . . . 30

POMONA . . . . . . . . . . . . . . . . . . . . . . 32

FLORA . . . . . . . . . . . . . . . . . . . . . . . 32

THUNDER IN THE GARDER . . . . . . . . . . . . . . 35

WHY DOST THOU STRUGGLE . . . . . . . . . . . . 37

TAPESTRY TREES . . . . . . . . . . . . . . . . . . 40

AN APOLOGY . . . . . . . . . . . . . . . . . . . . 42

MARCH . . . . . . . . . . . . . . . . . . . . . . . 45

APRIL . . . . . . . . . . . . . . . . . . . . . . . . 46

MAY . . . . . . . . . . . . . . . . . . . . . . . . . 48

JUNE . . . . . . . . . . . . . . . . . . . . . . . . . 49

JULY . . . . . . . . . . . . . . . . . . . . . . . . . 50

AUGUST . . . . . . . . . . . . . . . . . . . . . . . 53

SEPTEMBER . . . . . . . . . . . . . . . . . . . . . 54

OCTOBER . . . . . . . . . . . . . . . . . . . . . . 56

NOVEMBER . . . . . . . . . . . . . . . . . . . . . 57

DECEMBER . . . . . . . . . . . . . . . . . . . . . . 58

JANUARY . . . . . . . . . . . . . . . . . . . . . . 60

FEBRUARY . . . . . . . . . . . . . . . . . . . . . . 61

SO MANY STORIES WRITTEN HERE . . . . . . . . . 62

SAD-EYED SOFT AND GREY . . . . . . . . . . . . . 65

THE ORCHARD . . . . . . . . . . . . . . . . . . . 66

THE FLOWERING ORCHARD . . . . . . . . . . . . . 66

SONG FROM 'THE LOVE OF ALCESTIS' . . . . . . . . 68

THE HAYSTACK IN THE FLOOD . . . . . . . . . . . 71

O FAR AWAY TO SEEK . . . . . . . . . . . . . . . . 77

FROM THE UPLAND TO THE SEA . . . . . . . . . . . 78

THE WOODPECKER . . . . . . . . . . . . . . . . . 80

THE LION . . . . . . . . . . . . . . . . . . . . . . 80

THE FOREST . . . . . . . . . . . . . . . . . . . . . 80

THE MUSIC FROM 'LOVE IS ENOUGH' . . . . . . . . 82

MINE AND THINE . . . . . . . . . . . . . . . . . . 85

FAIR WEATHER AND FOUL . . . . . . . . . . . . . 86

MAY GROWN A-COLD . . . . . . . . . . . . . . . . 89

OUR HANDS HAVE MET . . . . . . . . . . . . . . . 90

THE MESSAGE OF THE MARCH WIND . . . . . . . . 92

FOR THE BED AT KELMSCOTT . . . . . . . . . . . . 95

Dante Gabriel Rossetti  LA PIA DE TOLOMMEI  1868-80

# INTRODUCTION

# THE SWEET DAYS DIE

POET, PAINTER, WRITER, WEAVER, DESIGNER OF EXQUISITE FURNITURE, BEAUTIFUL WALLPAPERS AND textiles, calligrapher, publisher, gardener, mediaevalist, revolutionary social reformer, romantic, energizer, the list of William Morris's accomplishments is long and extraordinarily varied, prompting Max Beerbohm to remark, rather sourly, in his old age:

> Of course he was a wonderful all-round man, but the act of walking
> round him always tired me.

In *The Sweet Days Die* we look at Morris the poet – the role which brought him the most fame in his lifetime, though not the one with which we now most obviously associate him. Today he is best-known for his intricate and lovely pattern designs but it was through his immensely popular poetry that he found his way into the hearts and drawing rooms of his vast Victorian public. Like Alfred, Lord Tennyson before him, he looked to the Middle Ages and the Arthurian legends for his inspiration and delivered to an already primed public poetry that was rich in colour and detail, lyrical and dramatic, full of the passion and romance of an earlier, chivalric time, in which they could escape from the sordid industrialization of their own age.

> 'To the jaded intellects of the present moment,' wrote Henry James in the *North American Review*, 'distracted with the strife of creeds and the conflicts of theories, it opens a glimpse into a world where they will be called upon neither to choose, to criticize, nor to believe, but simply to feel, to look, and to listen.'

Morris's poetic output was considerable. Despite the fact that his first collection, *The Defence of Guenevere*, published in 1858 when he was only twenty-four, aroused little critical excitement beyond his own circle of ardent admirers, he continued determinedly and his third volume, *The Earthly Paradise*, enjoyed immense success, as did his other long narrative poems, *The Death of Jason* and *Sigurd the Volsung*, which were based on classical myth and Icelandic saga. His prominence as a poet is demonstrated by the fact that he was offered the position of Poet Laureate on the death of Tennyson in 1892, but he declined the honour, as he had the Professorship of Poetry at Oxford University, offered in succession to Matthew Arnold in 1877. It was revolution rather than romance that occupied him increasingly in his later years and he found a fresh outlet for his literary energy and enthusiasm in the new-born Socialist movement, producing polemical works like *News from Nowhere* and expressing his indignation in poems like 'Mine and Thine' *(page 85)*.

His longer poems are little read today. Partly this is because the modern appetite is nourished on short, striking stanzas, which detonate swiftly. We no longer have the patience for the long fuse of an epic and we are no longer steeped in the chivalric tradition of Malory and Froissart. *The Earthly Paradise*, with its stately Chaucerian structure, is daunting and it has to be said that, despite the vividly evoked dream-like atmosphere, there is a certain monotony – of which Morris approved – to the regularity of the rhythm. For Morris, who was always engaged on several simultaneous projects, believed that:

> If a chap can't compose an epic poem while he is weaving a tapestry
> he had better shut up

This selection of his shorter lyrics demonstrate Morris's deep love of landscape, his strong feeling for history and his extraordinary gift for imaginative tale-telling which make him, at his best, a very beguiling poet indeed. The twelve beautiful and concentrated poems for the months convey his instinctive feeling for nature and season while also communicating personal life and pain. His first biographer, J W Mackail, writing in 1899, soon after Morris's death, chose not to dwell on the difficult emotional triangle formed by Morris, his wife Jane and the Pre-Raphaelite poet and painter Dante Gabriel Rossetti, but suggests that 'There is an autobiography so delicate and so outspoken that it must needs be left to speak for itself' in these poems.

In poems like 'The Haystack in the Flood' *(page 71)* he invokes the life of the Middle Ages, but he does not idealize it. The sense of beauty, always so prominent and visually explored in Morris's work, is almost overwhelmed by the sense of crisis and violence. He uses short, simple, definite words, arranged in clear patterns and colours, like his designs.

W. B. Yeats, who much admired Morris, declared with approval that he made his poetry 'out of unending pictures of a happiness that is often what a child might imagine, and always a happiness that sets mind and body at ease.' Certainly his love of the Middle Ages and deep response to nature were developed in his privileged childhood. His father, who had made his wealth effortlessly through a fortunate investment in a Devon mining firm, was a keen mediaevalist and designed a coat of arms for the family. He installed them in Woodford Hall, a Palladian mansion surrounded by a fifty acre park and farm, through which Morris, at seven, would trot on his pony, romantically attired in a miniature suit of armour. He was a dreamy, delicate child, who fed his imagination on Sir Walter Scott's *Waverly* novels, and liked nothing better than to ride beneath the ancient hornbeams of Epping Forest or trot round the local Essex churches, storing up the details of their medieval architecture and design.

Oxford, still largely a medieval city of romantic turrets, coiling staircases and graceful spires, delighted him when he arrived at Exeter College in 1852. There he made the friends who were to found the Firm with him, notably Edward Burne-Jones, and there, in the humble surroundings of her father's stable, he met his future wife, Jane Burden. Significantly, it was Rossetti who 'found' her. He called her 'a stunner' and all accounts agree on her strange, haunting loveliness which Rossetti was to idealize and iconoclize as the embodiment of Pre-Raphaelite beauty. However, Rossetti was deeply involved with his earlier muse,

Elizabeth Siddall, and it was Morris who seized the chivalric opportunity of rescuing this damsel from the dragon of poverty. They were married on 26 April 1859 in Oxford. No member of the Morris family was present, nor was Rossetti there. After a six week continental honeymoon, the couple returned to live in Red House – the 'small Palace of Art of my own' that Morris had commissioned for them in the Kent countryside.

The furnishing of Red House directed the Firm's distinctive style of craftsmanship. Morris was in revolt against the great tidal wave of industrialization and the shoddiness and greed he saw all around him.

> 'Have nothing in your houses that you do not know to be useful, or
> believe to be beautiful,' he insisted.

The paradox of course was that only the rich could afford the beautiful objects he designed. He may have greeted them gruffly in his blue worker's shirt, round hat, dirty hands and the impatient air of a busy man torn from something he would much rather be doing, but his bohemian behaviour only fuelled the aristocratic demand.

Henry James found him an impressive figure:

> 'He is short, burly, corpulent, very careless and unfinished in his dress. He has
> a very loud voice and a nervous restless manner and a perfectly unaffected
> and business-like address. His talk is wonderfully to the point and remarkable
> for clear good sense . . . He's an extraordinary example, in short, of a delicate
> sensitive genius and taste, saved by a perfectly healthy body and temper.'

The early years of married life were radiantly happy for Morris. His two daughters were born, the Firm flourished, but then two things happened to change everything. Burne-Jones was ill, forcing the relocation of the firm to Queen Square in London, and Elizabeth Siddall, long a laudanum addict, committed suicide, leaving Rossetti free to pursue Janey once more. She began to sit for Rossetti and soon they were lovers. Morris appears never to have blamed Rossetti or his wife, but he felt the betrayal keenly and his inner anguish and lonely regrets are reflected in a number of spare, painfully honest poems, including 'Why Dost Thou Struggle?' *(page 37)*, which were never published in his lifetime.

In fact, in a conventional age, Morris behaved with generous unconventionality, sharing the annual rent of £60 on Kelmscott Manor in Oxfordshire with Rossetti, to provide a place where for part of the year Janey and Rossetti could live together.

He sought solace in work and threw himself into politics. His shift from romantic to revolutionary is not as eccentric as it might seem. He was acutely aware that his own comfortable circumstances derived originally from the poorly rewarded toil of faraway Devon miners who worked in appalling conditions, and he was constantly alive to the social injustice and inequality he saw all around him. However, while tirelessly striving for socialist reform, he continued to live a comfortable capitalist life with a well staffed London house and spacious country retreat at Kelmscott. He continued to write poetry too and here we present a selection, illustrated with paintings by his Pre-Raphaelite friends, which exactly complement the visual intensity, rich glowing colours, leisurely movement and repeated decorative motifs of his work – for much of Morris's writing is really picture.

Towards the end of his life, Morris embarked on a new range of ambitious activities: he started the Kelmscott Press, began translating Icelandic sagas and made several long journeys to Iceland. For Morris, the man of means who hardly needed to earn a living, work had to be a pleasure rather than a duty. He rose early to teach himself new techniques, he packed it all in by doing at least two things at once, and he was fuelled by his strong enthusiasm, his romantic vision and his keen sense of social justice. When he died on 3 October 1896, aged 62, one of his doctors declared the cause of death was 'simply being William Morris and having done more work than most ten men'.

PAMELA TODD 1996

# CHRIST KEEP THE HOLLOW LAND

Through the sweet spring-tide,
When the apple-blossoms bless
The lowly bent hill side.

Christ keep the Hollow Land
All the summer-tide;
Still we cannot understand
Where the waters glide;

Only dimly seeing them
Coldly slipping through
Many green-lipp'd cavern mouths,
Where the hills are blue.

John William Waterhouse    A Song of Springtime

Ford Madox Brown   THE HAYFIELD   1855-6

# Summer Dawn

PRAY BUT ONE PRAYER FOR ME 'TWIXT THY CLOSED LIPS,
   Think but one thought of me up in the stars.
The summer night waneth, the morning light slips,
   Faint and grey 'twixt the leaves of the aspen, betwixt the cloud-bars,
That are patiently waiting there for the dawn:
   Patient and colourless, though Heaven's gold
Waits to float through them along with the sun.
Far out in the meadows, above the young corn,
   The heavy elms wait, and restless and cold
The uneasy wind rises; the roses are dun;
Through the long twilight they pray for the dawn,
Round the lone house in the midst of the corn.
   Speak but one word to me over the corn,
   Over the tender, bow'd locks of the corn.

SPRING WENT ABOUT THE WOODS TO-DAY,
The soft-foot winter-thief,
And found where idle sorrow lay
'Twixt flower and faded leaf.

She looked on him, and found him fair
For all she had been told;
She knelt adown beside him there,
And sang of days of old.

His open eyes beheld her nought,
Yet 'gan his lips to move;
But life and deeds were in her thought,
And he would sing of love.

So sang they till their eyes did meet,
And faded fear and shame;
More bold he grew, and she more sweet,
Until they sang the same.

Until, say they who know the thing,
Their very lips did kiss,
And Sorrow laid abed with Spring
Begat an earthly bliss.

# **F**AIR IS THE WORLD, NOW AUTUMN'S WEARING,

And the sluggard sun lies long abed;
Sweet are the days, now winter's nearing,
And all winds feign that the wind is dead.

Dumb is the hedge where the crabs hang yellow,
Bright as the blossoms of the spring;
Dumb is the close where the pears grow mellow,
And none but the dauntless redbreasts sing.

Fair was the spring, but amidst his greening
Grey were the days of the hidden sun;
Fair was the summer, but overweening,
So soon his o'er-sweet days were done.

Come then, love, for peace is upon us,
Far off is failing, and far is fear,
Here where the rest in the end hath won us,
In the garnering tide of the happy year.

Come from the grey old house by the water,
Where, far from the lips of the hungry sea,
Green groweth the grass o'er the field of the
    slaughter,
And all is a tale for thee and me.

## Verses for Pictures

### Day

I AM DAY; I BRING AGAIN
Life and glory, Love and pain:
Awake, arise! from death to death
Through  me the World's tale quickeneth.

### Spring

Spring am I, too soft of heart
Much to speak ere I depart:
Ask the Summer-tide to prove
The abundance of my love.

### Summer

Summer looked for long am I:
Much shall change or e'er I die.
Prithee take it not amiss
Though I weary thee with bliss.

### Autumn

Laden Autumn here I stand
Worn of heart, and weak of hand:
Nought but rest seems good to me,
Speak the word that sets me free.

### Winter

I am Winter, that do keep
Longing safe amidst of sleep:
Who shall say if I were dead
What should be remembered?

### Night

I am Night: I bring again
Hope of pleasure, rest from pain:
Thoughts unsaid 'twixt Life and Death
My fruitful silence quickeneth.

18

Evelyn de Morgan   THE CADENCE OF AUTUMN

# DRAWING NEAR THE LIGHT

Lo, WHEN WE WADE THE TANGLED WOOD,

In haste and hurry to be there,

Nought seem its leaves and blossoms good,

For all that they be fashioned fair.


But looking up, at last we see

The glimmer of the open light,

From o'er the place where we would be:

Then grow the very brambles bright.


So now, amidst our day of strife,

With many a matter glad we play,

When once we see the light of life

Gleam through the tangle of to-day.


C.H.W. (English School)  A CLEARING IN THE WOODS  1887

### THE BRIARWOOD

**T**HE FATEFUL SLUMBER FLOATS AND FLOWS

About the tangle of the rose;

But lo! the fated hand and heart

To rend the slumberous curse apart!

### THE GARDEN COURT

The maiden pleasance of the land

Knoweth no stir of voice or hand,

No cup the sleeping waters fill,

The restless shuttle lieth still.

### THE COUNCIL ROOM

The threat of war, the hope of peace,

The Kingdom's peril and increase

Sleep on, and bide the latter day,

When Fate shall take her chain away

### THE ROSEBOWER

Here lies the hoarded love, the key

To all the treasure that shall be;

Come fated hand the gift to take,

And smite this sleeping world awake.

Sir Edward Burne-Jones   THE ROSE BOWER from 'The Briar Rose Series   1870-90

**TREACHEROUS SCENT, O THORNY SIGHT,**

O tangle of world's wrong and right,

What art thou 'gainst my armour's gleam

But dusky cobwebs of a dream?


Beat down, deep sunk from every gleam

Of hope, they lie and dully dream;

Men once, but men no more, that Love

Their waste defeated hearts should move.


Here sleeps the world that would not love!

Let it sleep on, but if He move

Their hearts in humble wise to wait

On his new-wakened fair estate.


O won at last is never late!

Thy silence was the voice of fate;

Thy still hands conquered in the strife;

Thine eyes were light; thy lips were life.

Sir Edward Burne-Jones   THE BRIAR WOOD   1869

25

# HOW THE WIND HOWLS THIS MORN

About the end of May,

And drives June on apace

To mock the world forlorn

And the world's joy passed away

And my unlonged-for face!

The world's joy passed away;

For no more may I deem

That any folk are glad

To see the dawn of day

Sunder the tangled dream

Wherein no grief they had.

Ah, through the tangled dream

Where others have no grief

Ever it fares with me

That fears and treasons stream

And dumb sleep slays belief

Whatso therein may be.

Sleep slayeth all belief

Until the hopeless light

Wakes at the birth of June

More lying tales to weave,

More love in woe's despite,

More hope to perish soon.

Draw not away thy hands, my love,
With wind alone the branches move,
And though the leaves be scant above
The Autumn shall not shame us.

Say; Let the world wax cold and drear,
What is the worst of all the year
But life, and what can hurt us, dear,
Or death, and who shall blame us?

Ah, when the summer comes again
How shall we say, we sowed in vain?
The root was joy, the stem was pain,
The ear a nameless blending.

The root is dead and gone, my love,
The stem's a rod our truth to prove;
The ear is stored for nought to move
Till heaven and earth have ending.

Ford Madox Brown   Byron's Dream

# TWO RED ROSES ACROSS THE MOON

**T**HERE WAS A LADY LIVED IN A HALL,
Large in the eyes, and slim and tall;
And ever she sung from noon to noon,
*Two red roses across the moon.*

There was a knight came riding by
In early spring, when the roads were dry;
And he heard that lady sing at the noon,
*Two red roses across the moon.*

Yet none the more he stopp'd at all,
But he rode a-gallop past the hall;
And left that lady singing at noon,
*Two red roses across the moon.*

Because, forsooth, the battle was set,
And the scarlet and blue had got to be met,
He rode on the spur till the next warm noon:–
*Two red roses across the moon.*

But the battle was scatter'd from hill to hill,
From the windmill to the watermill;
And he said to himself, as it near'd the noon,
*Two red roses across the moon.*

You scarce could see for the scarlet and blue,
A golden helm or a golden shoe;
So he cried, as the fight grew thick at the noon,
*Two red roses across the moon!*

Verily then the gold bore through
The huddled spears of the scarlet and blue;
And they cried, as they cut them down at the noon,
*Two red roses across the moon!*

I trow he stopp'd when he rode again
By the hall, though draggled sore with the rain;
And his lips were pinch'd to kiss at the noon
*Two red roses across the moon.*

Under the may she stoop'd to the crown,
All was gold, there was nothing of brown;
And the horns blew up in the hall at noon,
*Two red roses across the moon.*

Sir Edward Burne-Jones   LAUS VENERIS   1873-75

## POMONA

**I**AM THE ANCIENT APPLE-QUEEN,

As once I was so am I now.

For evermore a hope unseen,

Betwixt the blossom and the bough.

Ah, where's the river's hidden Gold!

And where the windy grave of Troy?

Yet come I as I came of old,

From out the heart of Summer's joy.

## FLORA

**I**AM THE HANDMAID OF THE EARTH,

I broider fair her glorious gown,

And deck her on her days of mirth

With many a garland of renown.

And while Earth's little ones are fain

And play about the Mother's hem,

I scatter every gift I gain

From sun and wind to gladden them.

Dante Gabriel Rossetti  VENUS VERTI CORDIA  1864-8

WHEN THE BOUGHS OF THE GARDEN
HANG HEAVY WITH RAIN
And the blackbird reneweth his song,
And the thunder departing yet rolleth again,
I remember the ending of wrong.

When the day that was dusk while his
death was aloof
Is ending wide-gleaming and strange
For the clearness of all things beneath the world's
roof,
I call back the wild chance and the change.

For once we twain sat through the hot afternoon
While the rain held aloof for a while,
Till she, the soft-clad, for the glory of June
Changed all with the change of her smile.

For her smile was of longing, no longer of glee,
And her fingers, entwined with mine own,
With caresses unquiet sought kindness of me
For the gift that I never had known.

Then down rushed the rain, and the voice of the
thunder
Smote dumb all the sound of the street,
And I to myself was grown nought but a wonder,
As she leaned down my kisses to meet.

That she craved for my lips that had craved her
so often,
And the hand that had trembled to touch,
That the tears filled her eyes I had hoped not to
soften
In this world was a marvel too much.

Sidney Harold Meteyard  VENUS AND ADONIS

It was dusk 'mid the thunder, dusk e'en as the night,
When first brake out our love like the storm,
But no night-hour was it, and back came the light
While our hands with each other were warm.

And her smile killed with kisses, came back as at first
As she rose up and led me along,
And out to the garden, where nought was athirst,
And the blackbird renewing his song.

Earth's fragrance went with her, as in the wet grass,
Her feet little hidden were set;
She bent down her head, 'neath the roses to pass,
And her arm with the lily was wet.

In the garden we wandered while day waned apace
And the thunder was dying aloof;
Till the moon o'er the minster-wall lifted his face,
And grey gleamed out the lead of the roof.

Then we turned from the blossoms, and cold were
    they grown:
In the trees the wind westering moved;
Till over the threshold back fluttered her gown,
And in the dark house was I loved.

# **W**HY DOST THOU STRUGGLE, STRIVE FOR VICTORY

Over my heart that loveth thine so well?
When Death shall one day have its will of thee
And to deaf ears thy triumph thou must tell.

Unto deaf ears or unto such as know
The hearts of dead and living wilt thou say:
A childish heart there loved me once, and lo
I took his love and cast his love away.

A childish greedy heart! yet still he clung
So close to me that much he pleased my pride
And soothed a sorrow that about me hung
With glimpses of his love unsatisfied –

And soothed my sorrow – but time soothed it too
Though ever did its aching fill my heart
To which the foolish child still closer drew
Thinking in all I was to have a part.

But now my heart grown silent of its grief
Saw more than kindness in his hungry eyes:
But I must wear a mask of false belief
And feign that nought I know his miseries.

I wore a mask, because though certainly
I loved him not, yet was there something soft
And sweet to have him ever loving me:
Belike it is I well-nigh loved him oft –

Nigh loved him oft, and needs must grant to him
Some kindness out of all he asked of me
And hoped his love would still hang vague and dim
About my life like half-heard melody.

He knew my heart and over-well knew this
And strove, poor soul, to pleasure me herein;
But yet what might he do some doubtful kiss
Some word, some look might give him hope to win.

Poor hope, poor soul, for he again would come
Thinking to gain yet one more golden step
Toward Love's shrine, and lo the kind speech dumb,
The kind look gone, no love upon my lip –

Yea gone, yet not my fault, I knew of love
But my love and not his; how could I tell
That such blind passion in him I should move?
Behold I have loved faithfully and well;

Love of my love so deep and measureless
O lords of the new world this too ye know

(*unfinished*)

Arthur Hughes   AURORA LEIGH'S DISMISSAL OF ROMNEY ('THE TRYST')   1860

### OAK

**I AM THE ROOF-TREE AND THE KEEL;**
I bridge the seas for woe and weal.

### FIR

High o'er the lordly oak I stand,
And drive him on from land to land.

### ASH

I heft my brother's iron bane;
I shaft the spear, and build the wain.

### YEW

Dark down the windy dale I grow,
The father of the fateful Bow.

### POPLAR

The war-shaft and the milking-bowl
I make, and keep the hay-wain whole

### OLIVE

The King I bless; the lamps I trim;
In my warm wave do fishes swim.

### APPLE-TREE

I bowed my head to Adam's will;
The cups of toiling men I fill.

### VINE

I draw the blood from out the earth;
I store the sun for winter mirth.

### ORANGE-TREE

Amidst the greenness of my night,
My odorous lamps hang round and bright.

### FIG-TREE

I who am little among trees
In honey-making mate the bees.

### MULBERRY-TREE

Love's lack hath dyed my berries red:
For Love's attire my leaves are shed.

### PEAR-TREE

High o'er the mead-flowers' hidden feet
I bear aloft my burden sweet.

### BAY

Look on my leafy boughs, the Crown
Of living song and dead renown!

Dante Gabriel Rossetti  DAY DREAM  1880

# AN APOLOGY

OF HEAVEN OR HELL I HAVE NO POWER TO SING
I cannot ease the burden of your fears,
Or make quick-coming death a little thing,
Or bring again the pleasure of past years,
Nor for my words shall ye forget your tears,
Or hope again for aught that I can say,
The idle singer of an empty day.

But rather, when aweary of your mirth,
From full hearts still unsatisfied ye sigh,
And, feeling kindly unto all the earth,
Grudge every minute as it passes by,
Made the more mindful that the sweet days die –
– Remember me a little then I pray,
The idle singer of an empty day.

The heavy trouble, the bewildering care
That weighs us down who live and earn our bread,
These idle verses have no power to bear;
So let me sing of names remembered,
Because they, living not, can ne'er be dead,
Or long time take their memory quite away
From us poor singers of an empty day.

Dreamer of dreams, born out of my due time,
Why should I strive to set the crooked straight?
Let it suffice me that my murmuring rhyme
Beats with light wing against the ivory gate,
Telling a tale not too importunate
To those who in the sleepy region stay,
Lulled by the singer of an empty day.

Folk say, a wizard to a northern king
At Christmas-tide such wondrous things did show,
That through one window men beheld the spring,
And through another saw the summer glow,
And through a third the fruited vines a-row,
While still, unheard, but in its wonted way,
Piped the drear wind of that December day.

So with this Earthly Paradise it is,
If ye will read aright, and pardon me,
Who strive to build a shadowy isle of bliss
Midmost the beating of the steely sea,
Where tossed about all hearts of men must be;
Whose ravening monsters mighty men shall slay,
Not the poor singer of an empty day.

*From* THE EARTHLY PARADISE

Sir Edward Burne-Jones   CHANT D'AMOUR   1868-77

Ford Madox Brown   'THE PRETTY BAA-LAMBS'   1851-9

## MARCH

**SLAYER OF THE WINTER, ART THOU HERE AGAIN?**
O welcome, thou that bring'st the summer nigh!
The bitter wind makes not thy victory vain,
Nor will we mock thee for thy faint blue sky.
Welcome, O March! whose kindly days and dry
Make April ready for the throstle's song,
Thou first redresser of the winter's wrong!

Yea, welcome March! and though I die ere June,
Yet for the hope of life I give thee praise,
Striving to swell the burden of the tune
That even now I hear thy brown birds raise,
Unmindful of the past or coming days;
Who sing: "O joy! a new year is begun:
What happiness to look upon the sun!"

Ah, what begetteth all this storm of bliss
But Death himself, who crying solemnly,
E'en from the heart of sweet Forgetfulness,
Bids us "Rejoice, lest pleasureless ye die.
Within a little time must ye go by.
Stretch forth your open hands, and while ye live
Take all the gifts that Death and Life may give."

O **FAIR MIDSPRING, BESUNG SO OFT AND OFT,**

How can I praise thy loveliness enow?

Thy sun that burns not, and thy breezes soft

That o'er the blossoms of the orchard blow,

The thousand things that 'neath the young leaves grow,

The hopes and chances of the growing year,

Winter forgotten long, and summer near.

When Summer brings the lily and the rose,

She brings us fear; her very death she brings

Hid in her anxious heart, the forge of woes;

And, dull with fear, no more the mavis sings.

But thou! thou diest not, but thy fresh life clings

About the fainting autumn's sweet decay,

When in the earth the hopeful seed they lay.

Ah! life of all the year, why yet do I

Amid thy snowy blossoms' fragrant drift,

Still long for that which never draweth nigh,

Striving my pleasure from my pain to sift,

Some weight from off my fluttering mirth to lift?

Now, when far bells are ringing, "Come again,

Come back, past years! why will ye pass in vain?"

Sir John Everett Millais   Spring (Apple Blossom)   1856-9

LOVE, THIS MORN WHEN THE SWEET NIGHTINGALE

Had so long finished all he had to say,

That thou hadst slept, and sleep had told his tale;

And midst a peaceful dream had stolen away

In fragrant dawning of the first of May,

Didst thou see aught? didst thou hear voices sing

Ere to the risen sun the bells 'gan ring?


For then methought the Lord of Love went by

To take possession of his flowery throne,

Ringed round with maids, and youths, and minstrelsy;

A little while I sighed to find him gone,

A little while the dawning was alone,

And the light gathered; then I held my breath,

And shuddered at the sight of Eld and Death.


Alas! Love passed me in the twilight dun,

His music hushed the wakening ousel's song;

But on these twain shone out the golden sun,

And o'er their heads the brown bird's tune was strong,

As shivering, 'twixt the trees they stole along;

None noted aught their noiseless passing by,

The world had quite forgotten it must die.

**JUNE, O JUNE, THAT WE DESIRED SO,**

Wilt thou not make us happy on this day?
Across the river thy soft breezes blow
Sweet with the scent of beanfields far away,
Above our heads rustle the aspens grey,
Calm is the sky with harmless clouds beset,
No thought of storm the morning vexes yet.

See, we have left our hopes and fears behind
To give our very hearts up unto thee;
What better place than this then could we find
By this sweet stream that knows not of the sea,
That guesses not the city's misery,
This little stream whose hamlets scarce have names,
This far-off, lonely mother of the Thames?

Here then, O June, thy kindness will we take;
And if indeed but pensive men we seem,
What should we do? thou wouldst not have us wake
From out the arms of this rare happy dream
And wish to leave the murmur of the stream,
The rustling boughs, the twitter of the birds,
And all thy thousand peaceful happy words.

# FAIR WAS THE MORN TO-DAY, THE BLOSSOM'S SCENT

Floated across the fresh grass, and the bees

With low vexed song from rose to lily went,

A gentle wind was in the heavy trees,

And thine eyes shone with joyous memories;

Fair was the early morn and fair wert thou,

And I was happy – Ah, be happy now!


Peace and content without us, love within

That hour there was, now thunder and wild rain

Have wrapped the cowering world, and foolish sin

And nameless pride have made us wise in vain;

Ah, love! although the morn shall come again,

And on new rose-buds the new sun shall smile,

Can we regain what we have lost meanwhile?


E'en now the west grows clear of storm and threat,

But midst the lightning did the fair sun die –

Ah, he shall rise again for ages yet,

He cannot waste his life; but thou and I?

Who knows if next morn this felicity

My lips may feel, or if thou still shalt live

This seal of love renewed once more to give?

Sir Edward Burne-Jones  GREEN SUMMER

William Holman Hunt   THE HIRELING SHEPHERD   1851

ACROSS THE GAP MADE BY OUR ENGLISH HINDS,

Amidst the Roman's handiwork, behold

Far off the long-roofed church; the shepherd binds

The withy round the hurdles of his fold

Down in the foss the river fed of old,

That through long lapse of time has grown to be

The little grassy valley that you see.


Rest here awhile, not yet the eve is still,

The bees are wandering yet, and you may hear

The barley mowers on the trenchèd hill,

The sheep-bells, and the restless changing weir,

All little sounds made musical and clear

Beneath the sky that burning August gives,

While yet the thought of glorious Summer lives.


Ah, love! such happy days, such days as these,

Must we still waste them, craving for the best,

Like lovers o'er the painted images

Of those who once their yearning hearts have blessed?

Have we been happy on our day of rest?

Thine eyes say "yes," but if it came again,

Perchance its ending would not seem so vain.

# O
## COME AT LAST, TO WHOM THE SPRINGTIDE'S HOPE

Looked for through blossoms, what hast thou for me?

Green grows the grass upon the dewy slope

Beneath thy gold-hung, grey-leaved apple-tree

Moveless, e'en as the autumn fain would be

That shades its sad eyes from the rising sun

And weeps at eve because the day is done.


What vision wilt thou give me, autumn morn,

To make thy pensive sweetness more complete?

What tale, ne'er to be told, of folk unborn?

What images of grey-clad damsels sweet

Shall cross thy sward with dainty noiseless feet?

What nameless shamefast longings made alive,

Soft-eyed September, will thy sad heart give?


Look long, O longing eyes, and look in vain!

Strain idly, aching heart, and yet be wise,

And hope no more for things to come again

That thou beheldest once with careless eyes!

Like a new-wakened man thou art, who tries

To dream again the dream that made him glad

When in his arms his loving love he had.

Sir John Everett Millais  Autumn Leaves  1856

# O

**LOVE, TURN FROM THE UNCHANGING SEA, AND GAZE**

Down these grey slopes upon the year grown old,

A-dying mid the autumn-scented haze,

That hangeth o'er the hollow in the wold,

Where the wind-bitten ancient elms enfold

Grey church, long barn, orchard, and red-roofed stead,

Wrought in dead days for men a long while dead.


Come down, O love; may not our hands still meet,

Since still we live to-day, forgetting June,

Forgetting May, deeming October sweet –

– O hearken, hearken! through the afternoon,

The grey tower sings a strange old tinkling tune!

Sweet, sweet, and sad, the toiling year's last breath,

Too satiate of life to strive with death.


And we too – will it not be soft and kind,

That rest from life, from patience and from pain,

That rest from bliss we know not when we find,

That rest from Love which ne'er the end can gain? –

– Hark, how the tune swells, that erewhile did wane!

Look up, love! – ah, cling close and never move!

How can I have enough of life and love?

# NOVEMBER

**ARE THINE EYES WEARY? IS THY HEART TOO SICK**
To struggle any more with doubt and thought,
Whose formless veil draws darkening now and thick
Across thee, e'en as smoke-tinged mist-wreaths brought
Down a fair dale to make it blind and nought?
Art thou so weary that no world there seems
Beyond these four walls, hung with pain and dreams?

Look out upon the real world, where the moon,
Half-way 'twixt root and crown of these high trees,
Turns the dread midnight into dreamy noon,
Silent and full of wonders, for the breeze
Died at the sunset, and no images,
No hopes of day, are left in sky or earth –
Is it not fair, and of most wondrous worth?

Yea, I have looked and seen November there;
The changeless seal of change it seemed to be,
Fair death of things that, living once, were fair;
Bright sign of loneliness too great for me,
Strange image of the dread eternity,
In whose void patience how can these have part,
These outstretched feverish hands, this restless heart?

# DEAD LONELY NIGHT AND ALL STREETS QUIET NOW,

Thin o'er the moon the hindmost cloud swims past

Of that great rack that brought us up the snow;

On earth strange shadows o'er the snow are cast;

Pale stars, bright moon, swift cloud make heaven so vast

That earth left silent by the wind of night

Seems shrunken 'neath the grey unmeasured height.


Ah! through the hush the looked-for midnight clangs!

And then, e'en while its last stroke's solemn drone

In the cold air by unlit windows hangs,

Out break the bells above the year foredone,

Change, kindness lost, love left unloved alone;

Till their despairing sweetness makes thee deem

Thou once wert loved, if but amidst a dream.


O thou who clingest still to life and love,

Though nought of good, no God thou mayst discern,

Though nought that is, thine utmost woe can move,

Though no soul knows wherewith thine heart doth yearn,

Yet, since thy weary lips no curse can learn,

Cast no least thing thou lovedst once away,

Since yet perchance thine eyes shall see the day.

Sir John Everett Millais  GLEN BIRNAM  1891

FROM THIS DULL RAINY UNDERSKY AND LOW,
This murky ending of a leaden day,
That never knew the sun, this half-thawed snow,
These tossing black boughs faint against the grey
Of gathering night, thou turnest, dear, away
Silent, but with thy scarce-seen kindly smile
Sent though the dusk my longing to beguile.

There, the lights gleam, and all is dark without!
And in the sudden change our eyes meet dazed –
O look, love, look again! the veil of doubt
Just for one flash, past counting, then was raised!
O eyes of heaven, as clear thy sweet soul blazed
On mine a moment! O come back again,
Strange rest and dear amid the long dull pain!

Nay, nay, gone by! though there she sitteth still,
With wide grey eyes so frank and fathomless –
Be patient, heart, thy days they yet shall fill
With utter rest – Yea, now thy pain they bless,
And feed thy last hope of the world's redress –
O unseen hurrying rack! O wailing wind!
What rest and where go ye this night to find?

**N**OON – AND THE NORTH-WEST SWEEPS THE EMPTY ROAD,

The rain-washed fields from hedge to hedge are bare;

Beneath the leafless elms some hind's abode

Looks small and void, and no smoke meets the air

From its poor hearth: one lonely rook doth dare

The gale, and beats above the unseen corn,

Then turns, and whirling down the wind is borne.


Shall it not hap that on some dawn of May

Thou shalt awake, and, thinking of days dead,

See nothing clear but this same dreary day,

Of all the days that have passed o'er thine head?

Shalt thou not wonder, looking from thy bed,

Through green leaves on the windless east a-fire,

That this day too thine heart doth still desire?


Shalt thou not wonder that it liveth yet,

The useless hope, the useless craving pain,

That made thy face, that lonely noontide, wet

With more than beating of the chilly rain?

Shalt thou not hope for joy new born again,

Since no grief ever born can ever die

Through changeless change of seasons passing by?

# So Many Stories Written Here

So Many Stories Written Here

And none among them but doth bear

Its weight of trouble and of woe!

Well may you ask why it is so;

For surely neither sour nor dull

In such a world, of fair things full,

Should folk be.

        Ah, my dears, indeed

My wisdom fails me at my need

To tell why tales that move the earth

Are seldom of content and mirth.

Yet think if it may come of this –

That lives fulfilled of ease and bliss

Crave not for aught that we can give,

And scorn the broken lives we live;

Unlike to us they pass us by,

A dying laugh their history.

But those that struggled sore, and failed

Had one thing left them, that availed

When all things else were nought

        E'en Love –

Whose sweet voice, crying as they strove,

Begat sweet pity, and more love still,

Waste places with sweet tales to fill;

Whereby we, living here, may learn

Our eyes toward very Love to turn,

And all the pain it bringeth meet

As nothing strange amid the sweet:

Whereby we too may hope to be

Grains in the great world's memory

Of pain endured, and nobleness

That life ill-understood doth bless.

Words over-grave and sad for you

Maybe: but rime will still be true

Unto my heart – most true herein

In wishing, dear hearts, you may win

A life of every ill so clear,

That little tale for folk to hear

It may be: yet so full of love,

That e'en these words your hearts may move,

Years and years hence, when unto me

Life is a waste and windless Sea.

*Written in a copy of*
The Earthly Paradise, *Dec. 25, 1870*

Arthur Hughes   Home from the Sea: A Mother's Grave

**S**AD-EYED AND SOFT AND GREY THOU ART, O MORN!

Across the long grass of the marshy plain

Thy west wind whispers of the coming rain,

Thy lark forgets that May is grown forlorn

Above the lush blades of the springing corn,

Thy thrush within the high elms strives in vain

To store up tales of spring for summer's pain –

Vain day, why wert thou from the dark night born?


O many-voiced strange morn, why must thou break

With vain desire the softness of my dream

Where she and I alone on earth did seem?

How hadst thou heart from me that land to take

Wherein she wandered softly for my sake

And I and she no harm of love might deem?

Charles March Gere   THE LADY OF GREY DAYS

# THE ORCHARD

**M**IDST BITTEN MEAD AND ACRE SHORN,

The world without is waste and worn,

But here within our orchard-close,

The guerdon of its labour shows.

O valiant Earth, O happy year

That mocks the threat of winter near,

And hangs aloft from tree to tree

The banners of the Spring to be.

# THE FLOWERING ORCHARD

### SILK EMBROIDERY

**L**O SILKEN MY GARDEN,

and silken my sky,

And silken my apple-boughs

hanging on high;

All wrought by the Worm

in the peasant carle's cot

On the Mulberry leafage

when summer was hot!

John Roddam Spencer-Stanhope PENELOPE

## Song from 'The Love of Alcestis

O Dwellers on the lovely earth,

Why will ye break your rest and mirth
To weary us with fruitless prayer;
Why will ye toil and take such care
For children's children yet unborn,
And garner store of strife and scorn
To gain a scarce-remembered name,
Cumbered with lies and soiled with shame?
And if the gods care not for you,
What is this folly ye must do
To win some mortal's feeble heart?
O fools! when each man plays his part,
And heeds his fellow little more
Than these blue waves that kiss the shore
Take heed of how the daisies grow.
O fools! and if ye could but know
How fair a world to you is given.

O brooder on the hills of heaven,
When for my sin thou drav'st me forth,
Hadst thou forgot what this was worth,
Thine own hand had made? The tears of men,
The death of threescore years and ten,
The trembling of the timorous race –
Had these things so bedimmed the place
Thine own hand made, thou couldst not know
To what a heaven the earth might grow
If fear beneath the earth were laid,
If hope failed not, nor love decayed.

Sir Edward Burne-Jones  Earth Mother  1882

# H

**AD SHE COME ALL THE WAY FOR THIS,**

To part at last without a kiss?

Yea, had she borne the dirt and rain

That her own eyes might see him slain

Beside the haystack in the floods?


Along the dripping leafless woods,

The stirrup touching either shoe,

She rode astride as troopers do;

With kirtle kilted to her knee,

To which the mud splash'd wretchedly;

And the wet dripp'd from every tree

Upon her head and heavy hair,

And on her eyelids broad and fair;

The tears and rain ran down her face.


By fits and starts they rode apace,

And very often was his place

Far off from her; he had to ride

Ahead, to see what might betide

## THE HAYSTACK IN THE FLOODS

When the roads cross'd; and sometimes, when

There rose a murmuring from his men,

Had to turn back with promises;

Ah me! she had but little ease;

And often for pure doubt and dread

She sobb'd, made giddy in the head

By the swift riding; while, for cold,

Her slender fingers scarce could hold

The wet reins: yea, and scarcely, too,

She felt the foot within her shoe

Against the stirrup: all for this,

To part at last without a kiss

Beside the haystack in the floods.


For when they near'd that old soak'd hay,

They saw across the only way

That Judas, Godmar, and the three

Red running lions dismally

Grinn'd from his pennon, under which,

In one straight line along the ditch,

They counted thirty heads.


Mary F Raphael  BRITOMART AND AMORET  1898

So then,
While Robert turn'd round to his men,
She saw at once the wretched end,
And, stooping down, tried hard to rend
Her coif the wrong way from her head,
And hid her eyes; while Robert said:
'Nay, love, 'tis scarcely two to one,
At Poictiers where we made them run
So fast – why, sweet my love, good cheer,
The Gascon frontier is so near,
Nought after this.'
　　　　　But, 'O,' she said,
'My God! my God! I have to tread
The long way back without you; then
The court at Paris; those six men;
The gratings of the Chatelet;

The swift Seine on some rainy day
Like this, and people standing by,
And laughing, while my weak hands try
To recollect how strong men swim.
All this, or else a life with him,
For which I should be damned at last,
Would God that this next hour were past!'

He answer'd not, but cried his cry,
'St. George for Marny!' cheerily;
And laid his hand upon her rein.
Alas! no man of all his train
Gave back that cheery cry again;
And, while for rage his thumb beat fast
Upon his sword-hilt, some one cast
About his neck a kerchief long,
And bound him.
　　　　　Then they went along
To Godmar; who said: 'Now, Jehane,
Your lover's life is on the wane
So fast, that, if this very hour
You yield not as my paramour,
He will not see the rain leave off –
Nay, keep your tongue from gibe and scoff,
Sir Robert, or I slay you now.'

She laid her hand upon her brow,
Then gazed upon the palm, as though

She thought her forehead bled, and – 'No.'

She said, and turn'd her head away,

As there were nothing else to say,

And everything were settled: red

Grew Godmar's face from chin to head:

'Jehane, on yonder hill there stands

My castle, guarding well my lands:

What hinders me from taking you,

And doing that I list to do

To your fair wilful body, while

Your knight lies dead?'

        A wicked smile

Wrinkled her face, her lips grew thin,

A long way out she thrust her chin:

'You know that I should strangle you

While you were sleeping; or bite through

Your throat, by God's help - ah!' she said,

'Lord Jesus, pity your poor maid!

For in such wise they hem me in,

I cannot choose but sin and sin,

Whatever happens: yet I think

They could not make me eat or drink,

And so should I just reach my rest.'

'Nay, if you do not my behest,

O Jehane! though I love you well,'

Said Godmar, 'would I fail to tell

All that I know.' 'Foul lies,' she said.

'Eh? lies my Jehane? by God's head,

At Paris folks would deem them true!

Do you know, Jehane, they cry for you,

"Jehane the brown! Jehane the brown!

Give us Jehane to burn or drown!" –

Eh - gag me, Robert! – sweet my friend,

This were indeed a piteous end

For those long fingers, and long feet,

And long neck, and smooth shoulders sweet;

An end that few men would forget

That saw it – So, an hour yet:

Consider, Jehane, which to take

Of life or death!'

        So, scarce awake,

Dismounting, did she leave that place,

And totter some yards: with her face

Turn'd upward to the sky she lay,

Her head on a wet heap of hay,

And fell asleep: and while she slept,

And did not dream, the minutes crept

Round to the twelve again; but she,

Being waked at last, sigh'd quietly,

And strangely childlike came, and said:

I will not.' Straightway Godmar's head,
As though it hung on strong wires, turn'd
Most sharply round, and his face burn'd.

For Robert – both his eyes were dry,
He could not weep, but gloomily
He seem'd to watch the rain; yea, too,
His lips were firm; he tried once more
To touch her lips; she reach'd out, sore
And vain desire so tortured them,
The poor grey lips, and now the hem
Of his sleeve brush'd them.
                                        With a start
Up Godmar rose, thrust them apart;
From Robert's throat he loosed the bands
Of silk and mail; with empty hands
Held out, she stood and gazed, and saw,
The long bright blade without a flaw
Glide out from Godmar's sheath, his hand
In Robert's hair; she saw him  bend

Back Robert's head; she saw him send
The thin steel down; the blow told well,
Right backward the knight Robert fell,
And moan'd as dogs do, being half dead,
Unwitting, as I deem: so then
Godmar turn'd grinning to his men,
Who ran, some five or six, and beat
His head to pieces at their feet.

Then Godmar turn'd again and said:
'So, Jehane, the first fitte is read!
    Take note, my lady, that your way
Lies backward to the Chatelet!'
She shook her head and gazed awhile
At her cold hands with a rueful smile,
As though this thing had made her mad.

This was the parting that they had
Beside the haystack in the floods.

Sir Joseph Noel Paton   THE BLUIDIE TRYST   1855

John Roddam Spencer-Stanhope   Love and the Maiden

# O FAR AWAY TO SEEK, CLOSE-HID FOR HEART TO FIND,

O hard to cast away, Impossible to bind!
A pain when sought and found, A pain when slipped away,
Yet by whatever name, Be nigh us, Love, today.

Sweet was the summer day, Before thou camest here,
But never sweet to me, And Death was drawing near!
Is it summer still? What meaneth the word Death,
What meaneth all the joy Thy mouth, Love, promiseth?

Wherefore must thou babble Of thy finding me alone?
What is this idle word, That thou may'st yet be gone?
Laugh, laugh, Love, as I laugh, When mine own love kisseth me
And saith no more of bliss Twixt lips and lips shall be.

O Love, thou hast slain time, How shall he live again?
We bless thy bitter wound, We bless thy sleepless pain –
Hope and fear slain each of each Doubt forgetting all he said
Death in some place forgotten Lingering, and half dead.

When my hand forgets her cunning I will loose thee, Love, and pray
– Ah and pray to what – For a never-ending day,
Where we may sit apart, Hapless, undying still,
With thoughts of the old story Our sundered hearts to fill.

**S**HALL WE WAKE ONE MORN OF SPRING,

Glad at heart of everything,

Yet pensive with the thought of eve?

Then the white house shall we leave,

Pass the wind-flowers and the bays,

Through the garth, and go our ways,

Wandering down among the meads

Till our very joyance needs

Rest at last; till we shall come

To that Sun-God's lonely home,

Lonely on the hillside grey,

Whence the sheep have gone away;

Lonely till the feast-time is,

When with prayer and praise of bliss,

Thither comes the country side.

There awhile shall we abide,

Sitting low down in the porch

By that image with the torch:

Thy one white hand laid upon

The black pillar that was won

From the far-off Indian mine;

And my hand nigh touching thine,

But not touching; and thy gown

Fair with spring-flowers cast adown

From thy bosom and thy brow.

There the south-west wind shall blow

**F**ROM THE UPLAND TO THE SEA

Through thine hair to reach my cheek,

As thou sittest, nor mayst speak,

Nor mayst move the hand I kiss

For the very depth of bliss;

Nay, nor turn thine eyes to me.

Then desire of the great sea

Nigh enow, but all unheard,

In the hearts of us is stirred,

And we rise, we twain at last,

And the daffodils downcast,

Feel thy feet and we are gone

From the lonely Sun-Crowned one.

Then the meads fade at our back,

And the spring day 'gins to lack

That fresh hope that once it had;

But we twain grow yet more glad,

And apart no more may go

When the grassy slope and low

Dieth in the shingly sand:

Then we wander hand in hand

By the edges of the sea,

And I weary more for thee

Than if far apart we were,

With a space of desert drear

'Twixt thy lips and mine, O love!

Ah, my joy, my joy thereof!

William Holman Hunt   OLD ENGLISH COASTS (STRAYED SHEEP)   1852

Briton Riviere   Una and the Lion   1880

# THE WOODPECKER

**I** **ONCE A KING AND CHIEF**
Now am the tree-bark's thief,
Ever 'twixt trunk and leaf
Chasing the prey.

# THE LION

**T**HE BEASTS THAT BE
In wood and waste,
Now sit and see,
Nor ride nor haste.

# THE FOREST

PEAR TREE
**B**Y WOODMAN'S EDGE I FAINT AND FAIL;
By craftsman's edge I tell the tale.

CHESTNUT-TREE
High in the wood, high o'er the hall,
Aloft I rise when low I fall.

OAK-TREE
Unmoved I stand what wind may blow.
Swift, swift before the wind I go.

# LOVE IS ENOUGH: IT GREW UP WITHOUT HEEDING

In the days when ye knew not its name nor its measure,

And its leaflets untrodden by the light feet of pleasure

Had no boast of the blossom, no sign of the seeding,

As the morning and evening passed over its treasure.


And what do ye say then? – That Spring long departed

Has brought forth no child to the softness and showers;

– That we slept, and we dreamed through the Summer of flowers;

We dreamed of the Winter, and waking dead-hearted

Found Winter upon us and waste of dull hours.


Nay, Spring was o'er happy and knew not the reason,

And Summer dreamed sadly, for she thought all was ended

In her fulness of wealth that might not be amended;

But this is the harvest and the garnering season,

And the leaf and the blossom in the ripe fruit are blended.


It sprang without sowing, it grew without heeding,

Ye knew not its name and ye knew not its measure,

Ye noted it not mid your hope and your pleasure;

There was pain in its blossom, despair in its seeding,

But daylong your bosom now nurseth its treasure.

*From* LOVE IS ENOUGH

John Melhuish Strudwick  'WHEN APPLES WERE GOLDEN AND SONGS WERE SWEET AND SUMMER HAD PASSED AWAY

82

# **M**INE AND THINE

*From a Flemish poem of the fourteenth century*

**T**WO WORDS ABOUT THE WORLD WE SEE,

And nought but Mine and Thine they be.

Ah! might we drive them forth and wide

With us should rest and peace abide;

All free, nought owned of goods and gear,

By men and women though it were.

Common to all all wheat and wine

Over the seas and up the Rhine.

No manslayer then the wide world o'er

When Mine and Thine are known no more.

Yea, God, well counselled for our health,

Gave all this fleeting earthly wealth

A common heritage to all,

That men might feed them therewithal,

And clothe their limbs and shoe their feet

And live a simple life and sweet.

But now so rageth greediness

That each desireth nothing less

Than all the world, and all his own;

And all for him and him alone.

Frederick Smallfield  EARLY LOVERS

85

**S**PEAK NOUGHT, MOVE NOT, BUT LISTEN, THE SKY IS FULL OF GOLD,

No ripple on the river, no stir in field or fold,

All gleams but nought doth glisten, but the far-off unseen sea.


Forget days past, heart broken, put all memory by!

No grief on the green hill-side, no pity in the sky,

Joy that may not be spoken fills mead and flower and tree.


Look not, they will not heed thee, speak not, they will not hear,

Pray not, they have no bounty, curse not, they may not fear,

Cower down, they will not heed thee; long-lived the world shall be.


Hang down thine head and hearken, for the bright eve mocks thee still:

Night trippeth on the twilight, but the summer hath no will

For woes of thine to darken, and the moon hath left the sea.


Hope not to tell thy story in the rest of grey-eyed morn,

In the dawn grown grey and rainy, for the thrush ere day is born

Shall be singing to the glory of the day-star mocking thee.

John William Waterhouse   MIRANDA, THE TEMPEST

Be silent, worn and weary, till their tyranny is past,
For the summer joy shall darken, and the wind wail low at last,
And the drifting rack and dreary shall be kind to hear and see.

Thou shalt remember sorrow, thou shalt tell all thy tale
When the rain fills up the valley, and the trees amid their wail
Think far beyond tomorrow, and the sun that yet shall be.

Hill-side and vineyard hidden, and the river running rough,
Toward the flood that meets the northlands, shall be rest for thee enough
For thy tears to fall unbidden, for thy memory to go free.

Rest then, when all moans round thee, and no fair sunlitten lie
Maketh light of sorrow underneath a brazen sky,
And the tuneful woe hath found thee, over land and over sea.

OCERTAINLY, NO MONTH THIS IS BUT MAY!

    Sweet earth and sky, sweet birds of happy song,

    Do make thee happy now, and thou art strong,

And many a tear thy love shall wipe away

And make the dark night merrier than the day,

    Straighten the crooked paths and right the wrong,

    And tangle bliss so that it tarry long.

Go cry aloud the hope the Heavens do say!


Nay what is this? and wherefore lingerest thou?

    Why sayest thou the sky is hard as stone?

    Why sayest thou the thrushes sob and moan?

Why sayest thou the east tears bloom and bough?

Why seem the sons of man so hopeless now?

    Thy love is gone, poor wretch, thou art alone!

OUR HANDS HAVE MET, OUR LIPS HAVE MET,

Our souls – who knows when the wind blows
How light souls drift mid longings set,
If thou forget'st, can I forget
The time that was not long ago?

Thou wert not silent then, but told
Sweet secrets dear – I drew so near
Thy shamefaced cheeks grown overbold,
That scarce thine eyes might I behold!
Ah was it then so long ago!

Trembled my lips and thou wouldst turn
But hadst no heart to draw apart,
Beneath my lips thy cheek did burn –
Yet no rebuke that I might learn;
Yea kind looks still, not long ago.

Wilt thou be glad upon the day
When unto me this love shall be
An idle fancy passed away,
And we shall meet and smile {and} say
"O wasted sighs of long ago!"

Wilt thou rejoice that thou hast set
Cold words, dull shows 'twixt hearts drawn close,
That cold at heart I live on yet,
Forgetting still that I forget
The priceless days of long ago?

Sir Edward Burne-Jones (at Wightwick Manor)   LOVE AMONG THE RUINS   1894

Sir Edward Burne-Jones   THE MARCH MARIGOLD   c1870

F**AIR NOW IS THE SPRING-TIDE, NOW EARTH
LIES BEHOLDING**

With the eyes of a lover, the face of the sun;
Long lasteth the daylight, and hope is enfolding
The green-growing acres with increase begun.

Now sweet, sweet it is through the land to be straying
'Mid the birds and the blossoms and the beasts
  of the field;
Love mingles with love, and no evil is weighing
On thy heart or mine, where all sorrow is healed.

From township to township, o'er down and by tillage
Fair, far have we wandered and long was the day;
But now cometh eve at the end of the village,
Where over the grey wall the church riseth grey.

There is wind in the twilight; in the white road
  before us
The straw from the ox-yard is blowing about;
The moon's rim is rising, a star glitters o'er us,
And the vane on the spire-top is swinging in doubt.

Down there dips the highway, toward the bridge
  crossing over
The brook that runs on to the Thames and the sea.
Draw closer, my sweet, we are lover and lover;
This eve art thou given to gladness and me.

Shall we be glad always? Come closer and hearken:
Three fields further on, as they told me down there,
When the young moon has set, if the March sky
  should darken,
We might see from the hill-top the great city's glare.

Hark, the wind in the elm-boughs! from London
  it bloweth,
And telleth of gold, and of hope and unrest;
Of power that helps not; of wisdom that knoweth,
But teacheth not aught of the worst and the best.

Of the rich men it telleth, and strange is the story
How they have, and they hanker, and grip far and wide;
And they live and they die, and the earth and its glory
Has been but a burden they scarce might abide.

Hark! the March wind again of a people is telling;
Of the life that they live there, so haggard and grim,
That if we and our love amidst them had been dwelling
My fondness had faltered, thy beauty grown dim.

This land we have loved in our love and our leisure
For them hangs in heaven, high out of their reach;
The wide hills o'er the sea-plain for them have
    no pleasure,
The grey homes of their fathers no story to teach.

The singers have sung and the builders have builded,
The painters have fashioned their tales of delight;
For what and for whom hath the world's book
    been gilded,
When all is for these but the blackness of night?

How long, and for what is their patience abiding?
How oft and how oft shall their story be told,
While the hope that none seeketh in darkness is hiding,
And in grief and in sorrow the world groweth old?

Come back to the inn, love, and the lights and the fire,
And the fiddler's old tune and the shuffling of feet;
For there in a while shall be rest and desire,
And there shall the morrow's uprising be sweet.

Yet, love, as we wend, the wind bloweth behind us,
And beareth the last tale it telleth to-night,
How here in the spring-tide the message shall find us;
For the hope that none seeketh is coming to light.

Like the seed of mid-winter, unheeded, unperished,
Like the autumn-sown wheat 'neath the snow lying
    green,
Like the love that o'ertook us, unawares and
    uncherished,
Like the babe 'neath thy girdle that groweth unseen;

So the hope of the people now buddeth and groweth,
Rest fadeth before it, and blindness and fear;
It biddeth us learn all the wisdom it knoweth;
It hath found us and held us, and biddeth us hear:

For it beareth the message: "Rise up on the morrow
And go on your ways toward the doubt and the strife:
Join hope to our hope and blend sorrow with sorrow,
And seek for men's love in the short days of life."

But lo, the old inn, and the lights and the fire,
And the fiddler's old tune and the shuffling of feet;
Soon for us shall be quiet and rest and desire,
And to-morrow's uprising to deeds shall be sweet.

THE WIND'S ON THE WOLD
And the night is a-cold,
And Thames runs chill
Twixt mead and hill,
But kind and dear
Is the old house here,
And my heart is warm
Midst winter's harm.
Rest, then and rest,
And think of the best
Twixt summer and spring
When all birds sing
In the town of the tree,
And ye lie in me
And scarce dare move
Lest earth and its love
Should fade away
Ere the full of the day.

I am old and have seen
Many things that have been,
Both grief and peace,
And wane and increase.
No tale I tell
Of ill or well,
But this I say,
Night treadeth on day,
And for worst and best
Right good is rest.

# Acknowledgements

Visitors of the Ashmolean Museum, Oxford, *page 63*.

Birmingham City Art Gallery, *page 44*.

Bridgeman Art Library, *pages 20, 27, 64 and 76*.

Christie's Images, *page 51*.

Christie's, London/Bridgeman Art Library, *page 69*.

Russell Cotes Art Gallery, Bournemouth/Bridgeman Art Library, *page 33*.

Faringdon Collection, Buscot, Oxon/Bridgeman Art Library, *page 23*.

Glasgow Museums: Art Gallery and Museum, Kelvingrove, *page 75*.

Lady Lever Art Gallery, Port Sunlight, (Board of Trustees of the National Museums and Galleries on Merseyside), Liverpool, *page 47*.

Laing Art Gallery, Newcastle-upon-Tyne/Bridgeman Art Library, *page 31*.

Maas Gallery/Bridgeman Art Library, *pages 25 and 80*.

Manchester City Art Galleries, *pages 2, 28, 52, 55, 59, 83 and 84*.

Metropolitan Museum of Art, New York, Alfred N. Punnett Endowment Fund, *page 43*.

The National Trust Photographic Library (from the de Morgan Foundation)/Cragside, *page 19*.

The National Trust Photographic Library (Derrick E. Witty)/Wightwick Manor, *page 91*.

Piccadilly Art Gallery/Bridgeman Art Library, *page 92*.

Sotheby's, London, *pages 13, 34, 70, 87 and cover*.

Spencer Museum of Art, University of Kansas, *page 6*.

Tate Gallery, London, *pages 14, 38 and 79*.

Victoria and Albert Museum, London/Bridgeman Art Library, *page 41*.

PICTURE RESEARCH: GABRIELLE ALLEN